STRAY CAT CAFE

DEAN MEREDITH

Copyright © 2017 Dean Meredith

ISBN: 978-1-925590-62-3
Published by Vivid Publishing
A division of Fontaine Publishing Group
P.O. Box 948, Fremantle
Western Australia 6959
www.vividpublishing.com.au

Cataloguing-in-Publication data is available from the National Library of Australia

All rights reserved. No part of this publication may be reproduced, stored in a retrieval system or transmitted in any form or by any means, electronic, mechanical, photocopying, recording or otherwise, without the prior written permission of the copyright holder. The information, views, opinions and visuals expressed in this publication are solely those of the author(s) and do not necessarily reflect those of the publisher.

So Real

Awake and dreaming
A cobweb dances
In the breeze of my breath
On a wind of cool jazz
Blown by immortal souls
Lost in eternal ether

Spirits sway in darkness
Writhing wraithlike
Whispering secret seduction
Licking pristine fangs
Eyes electric
Crazy and gone
Blind but seeing so much

Numb and feeling
Every sweet rapturous note
Tasting the pungent intensity
Of pleasurable pain
A rush so pure
Like a speeding
Brakeless express

Harlequin hipsters
Tripping phantom lights
Luminous lung caverns
Swirling smoky spectres
Drifting to heaven
Minds mesmerized
By mystic musicians

Soft Shiraz drapes hang
Like giant gypsy skirts
A tired old clock
Keeps perfect beat
Heavy lids slowly close
Chalky grey ash pauses
Teeters and falls

Shards of gaseous sunlight
Silently creep through cracks
Glass shatters
With muffled screams
And street noise staggers
Through a glaring door

Ol' Misery

Ol' misery's a friend o' mine
We often meet for cheese 'n' wine
Sometimes loneliness comes along
Worn out shoes 'n' a bran' new song

Smoke 'n' joke 'n' bluff our way
Rememberin' when them queens did stay
Films 'n' photos 'n' books in our heads
'N' love stained sheets on unmade beds

Bottle Brush

By the bristling bottle brush
He lied to lay his lovely lush

And drunken dreams did darkly dwell
With webs of words in a whiskey well

His fairy-floss hair white like cotton
Her itching scratch ne'er forgotten

To Josephine

Home in four days
My Crème Caramel
Don't bathe Chéri
My Oyster Naturél

Polarity

Day becomes night
Night becomes day
Dark becomes light
Blue turns to grey

Good becomes evil
Heaven becomes hell
Angel becomes devil
In darkness to dwell

Serf becomes lord
Good goes bad
Happy gets bored
Changes to sad

Up goes down
In walks out
Certain of nothing
All in doubt

First becomes last
Outside moves in
Future the past
Sanctity – sin

Blind regain sight
Broken mend
Black turns white
Beginnings end

Maybe

Maybe she's all I'm not?
Maybe she's all I can be?
Maybe she's her and
Maybe she's me?

Owed to Leonard

Let's build a dream
And fence it in white
But leave a few gaps
To let through the night

The Letter

And yes I smelled the paper
Of the letter that you wrote me
It started with a saying
That at first I couldn't follow
But then I understood
Or thought I did

And it was you
Giving part of you to me
And every part is sacred
Vulnerable and true
I love beauty and
That's all I see in you

The Cold Old Forest

Snowflakes softly falling, falling
Wind and wolves calling, calling
Pine trees pointing soaring, soaring
Brown bears snoozing snoring, snoring
Field mice scurry hiding, hiding
Wild cat chasing sliding, sliding
Fat moon smiling beaming, beaming
Winter's breath steaming, steaming

Dear Queen

I shall send
Each night at eight
A little kiss
To your rusty gate
Finding it locked
And him being small
He won't be able
To climb your wall
Your letter box
His only hope
His resting place
An envelope

Stray Cat Café

On a dreary day too poor for a name,
He dragged himself down to the little café,
Flat white and a paper, always the same,
He fumbled for coins and something to say,
His hand struck silver, but his mind no gold,
The coffee machine frothed a mocking hiss,
His soft fingers touched the counter so cold,
And there she was, a sunny shining miss,
All glowing with life and lighter than air,
Pink lemonade cheeks and strawberry lips,
A chef's hat hiding her blonde wistful hair,
Uniform jealously guarding her hips,
As soon as she smiled, his fears departed,
And that praise God was how it all started.

To a Poetess

I wonder if your words are free
And if my inner eye might see
Climbing up your fruit filled tree
A thorny devil much like me

Love & Lust

On a hazy night with half a moon
Running late but still too soon
Her nectar smooth, gold and sweet
Picture perfect and soul complete

Music soft and thoughts set free
Curling smoke and hearts that see
Silken touch and seductive look
Wanting her open like a book

Gentle kisses, cheeks and lips
Hands exploring curves and hips
Passions mounting with desire
Tongues tasting licks of fire

Seeing beauty, feeling more
No idea what's in-store
Press and rub, jeans expand
Zipper down, enter hand

Knowing eyes and wicked grin
Sensual mouth made for sin
Slippery, sliding, warm and wet
Too much pleasure to ever forget

She took him all and ate it up
Wouldn't allow a drink from her cup
He writhed and throbbed, ready to burst
Needing so badly to quench her thirst

Both in tune, both in beat
Wanting jazz and steamy heat
Flawless French and sultry hair
Love and lust, what a pair

Flowers

Today I looked for flowers
I had roses in mind
But all I found were poppies
My first thought was death
And then remembrance
But next came courage
And self-sacrifice
And the eternal flame
And love and peace
I wanted to give you a flower
I wanted to give you a bunch
I wanted to fill your car
I wanted to fill your life
With flowers and colour and beauty
Then I realised that
God has already done it
And I'm no God
I'm hardly even a man
And you are lovelier than any garden
And I unworthy to weed around you
And yet my acid rain
Cannot damage your innocent petals
They seem to thrive on it
As though you were made
For nuclear winter
As though my mushroom cloud
Was just a necessary part
Of your nurturing nature
I found my fragrant flower
Beauty blessed and heaven's scent

Hooray for Milk!

For standing up to plate
And his cronies -
Plain and peanut butter
Then along came marmalade

The Taming of the Beast

Oh I love you dearly miss
Though you frustrate me so
I am full of faith in you
As thoughts go to and fro

I so old and you so young
Who'd have thought it twice?
That fire could learn patience
From melting blocks of ice

And though I pull and struggle
As you run me round the ring
Now I know you mean no harm
Only praise for you I sing

And when I feel the sting of whip
And bits between my teeth
I'll understand in your firm hand
Love looms in veins beneath

You will tame this brutish beast
And so grateful will he be
When you ride upon his back
Such wonders both shall see

Wanted

So what do you want?
I just want someone who loves me
Oh is that all?
Well they need to really love me
That's better
It needs to be a bit difficult

Butterfly & Bee

He offered imperfection
And said it was for free
I settled for deception
Knew he wouldn't see

He could have if he wanted
But his eyes were just for me
I found it quite confronting
Yet chose not to break free

Then he went and spoiled it
I wished he'd let me be
But he was such an idiot
And worried that I'd flee

He makes pretty music
Lives in big old tree
Thinks I maybe magic
I butterfly - him bee

Silly Little Dreams

Barely breathing
Staying alive
Holding on
Trying so hard
To survive
Silly little dreams

Hooked

I've been lurking down here deep,
In cold constant night,
Sometimes I swim up,
And spy the surface shapes,
Their silhouettes beneath the light,
I don't get too close,
I heed the warnings,
Of the old and gone,
And tales of terror,
Of monsters from land,
But when I saw that shining dancing hook,
It was all I could see,
And a strange hypnotic hunger,
Had its way with me,
I gobbled your pearl - shell and all,
In one almighty piercing bite,
And darting pain through bleeding gum,
Soon replaced my dreamy delight,
As quick as all my wits awoke,
I dove and dove with no look back,
And swam and swam,
And felt the tearing steel on mouth,
And pull of line so long unending,
Barb in flesh with tightness bending,
Gills all gasping open gaping,
Fins so sore from mad descending,
Cheek all sliced from constant pulling,
I feel my struggle slowly ending,
Nervous bloody pulses sending,
Slipping back I think not knowing,

Dragging drifting redness flowing,
Sudden surges send me thrashing,
Lashing out at fears of going,
Off to die and then be eaten,
Tender mercilessly beaten,
Hung up high with eyes all popping,
Dripping dry in wind sails flapping,
Pecking birds squawking clapping,
Licking beaks ready for feasting,
Humans hurriedly steer returning,
To silent towns softly sleeping,
But I'm awake and still in water,
While you're celebrating laughing,
One last surge I'm not done yet,
With all the crazy strength left in me,
I zip and zing like liquid lightning,
Snapping line too taught from tightening,
I'm free I'm free and fleeing swiftly,
Feeling lightness now upon me,
I wear my body piercing proudly,
And pray one day to find you paddling,
So I may turn the tide my captor,
And tear the page from your last chapter.

Hello Jackie O

Don't be so hard
You do it too
With black beating shirt
And hairy dark hue
Don't mock her parade
Her self-esteem fair
Without her you're nothing
No-one, nowhere
Allow her a moment
And help her to dare
To feel like someone
That really is there
She'll wear what she wants
And do as she please
You have no right
To snicker or tease
For she is a lady
And she is the sea
You are but sand
That she has let be

Nothing

He sat and stared
And thought of nothing
Eyes all searching
Seeing nothing
Blindly blinking
Thinking nothing
Words and papers poised
For anything
Into space he surely drifted
Floating dreaming waiting
Nothing
Hearing squeaking
That was something
Someone scribbling
While he rusted
But it was nothing
Whiteboard blank
Erased and dusted

Going Things

And when you're gone
I'll have one less thing
And until all my other things go
I'll have them
And when they're all gone
I'll have nothing
Which is at least a word?

Indelible

I felt your bones
The day the train crushed them
A couple of bumps in time
Then paralysed silence
And my itinerant mind
Just could not leave the scene

Us

Once there was just us
The little miss and I
Then along came you
And it was us
Including you
Then you left
And it was just me
And little miss again
I am me
And you are you
And she is she
And we are as we are
And as we think
We're meant to be

Losing My Rhyme

A sense of humour
What rhymes with that?
Cancer!
A dignified death
What rhymes with that?
Blow-job!
Worthless wasted life
What rhymes with that?
Harlots and trouble
That's what!
And then ...
How about whores in heaven?
What of them?
Well about beating them
Are you referring to violence?
No I'm talking about
Getting there first
Oh!
It's not a race you know
Then why is it called
The human race
I don't know
But you're educated
You're supposed to know
Everything!
What I do know is
I've lost my rhyme
And my reason
Damn you!
Now where was I?

Who was I?
Another time!
Oh yes – heaven
What rhymes with that?
Stale bread or
A crooked number
Take your pick
I'll have the latter please
Numerology you know
Indeed ...
And then ...
What rhymes with boredom?
Nothing!

Symptomatic

It's a weak dry cough
And a head full of cement
It's a little bit of phlegm
Every now and then
A throat like a cheese grater
Shaving raw testicles
A body like someone else's
Old shrivelling slowly dying
Like a slug in an oven
Its red onion eyes
With lemon peel lids
It's the short sharp tip
Of a breath full of fear
Like inhaling needles
On Everest

Seeing Me

Sure she's ugly
But she's someone's daughter
Someone's little girl
And to her daddy
She's a princess
We're all ugly
In some way
How we look
The way we see
And is that wrong?
I don't know
Who made me judge?
Oh yes ...
That would have been me

What Is Left Unsaid

We carefully speak
Around the painful loss
As though the words
Form a distinct outline
Of what is gone
Like a graphic photo negative
The background defines the image
The darkness focuses the light
The blackness surrounds the white
Out of respect
We avoid mention
Of the dead

Hotel

Red dress
Spotlight
Hair black
Skin white
Cold keys
Touch light

Red hair
Fire light
Black tie
Shirt white
New news
Uptight

Red chair
Hot light
Bookshelf
Upright
Window
Shut tight

Red door
Cool night
Rainbow
Streetlight
Gold dust
Too bright

Pair of Shoes

If you walked a mile
In one of my shoes
And I walked a mile
In one of yours
I wonder
If we'd finish up together
Or knot

Oh Sylvia

If only you knew
Perhaps you do
How much I feel
For you
It's true
You left too soon
But left a clue
Or two
You left a few
It's just so sad
But nothing new
As they left you
You left us too

In Memory of Lost Words

Honesty renders memory poor
Words they flee so easily
As if through ever open door
Wicked winds will them free
But they're mine made by me
Without my mind they'd not exist
My inner eye gave life to thee
Silently they sink into the mist
Shadows left by sun then moon
Alone to find and feel their way
Orphaned from my weeping womb
Not knowing whether night or day
Go my children and seek the light
Truth will guide to where it's bright

Two Way Mirror

Oh ugliness
This mask
That grows upon me
With age
Dear friend
Such a gift you give
The virtuous vision
Of the sage
To see the truth
The curse though
Is it sees you too

Water Finds Its Way

Just as a river must flow from high to low
Life's journey is much the same
And tho we grow from small to tall
The path is the secret to the game
When all is done and wicked wisdom shows
True happiness knows not highs or lows
For pure joy is merry and just content to be
And this is all that time who takes so much
But in return would have you know
And as a final gift give unto thee

Am I Toasted?

Will I crumble?
And fall apart?
Or am I just
Crumby and stale
Cheap white bread
With a brownish hue
Even the cheesy bits
Are a bit flaky
And the butter
Spread too thick

Black and Blue

Why is the sky?
So dark tonight
Like a shroud
Waiting to fall
On all below
Elms of lime
And lemony gold
A lip red light
All alluring
On the corner
What's that black?
Is it blue black?
Or that new black
Black on black
Anything
To get her back

Who Knows?

I loved her once
But that was long ago
She loved me too
How much I'll never know

I love her still
But had to let her go
I always will
How much she'll never know

Raw

Yeah
Take my bloodied meat
And throw it
Against the wall
And hammer a steak
Into it
Before it falls
And look on
As it tries
To crawl
Away
And see
The sap run dry
And watch it die
Brown and grey
Warm then cool
And hear it say
Nothing at all
Not a single sound
And admire
The way
It goes
Quiet at the end
And smell death
In the room
And wonder why
There is no gloom
Its shades of white
And never black
Except long after

The attack
And losses counted
Trophies mounted
Darkness only comes
When we turn out
The light

Down Under

Death came
As a gardener
With fork and spade
He smiled and seemed
Happy to see me
Wish I could say the same
But I was ready
My work was done
I'd sowed my seed
And lived too long
So where's the fire?
You see
I had flames in mind
Oh that's below
He said
So I said
Lead the way
So he did
And before too long
We were deep underground
In a torch lit tunnel
Winding like a serpent
It took some time
He was in a hurry
I wasn't
Then there we were
It wasn't like I'd imagined
Hell it was huge
And everyone was there

Ghosts of the Sea

She is the moon
And he is the sea
Without her he knows
He ceases to be
The sirens he hears
Were all sent by she
They are just fears
Ghosts that he flees
Wrecks on the beds
Shells of his seas

Unwanted

Sunday came as an Uncle
He'd been away
Doing time

Brought with him a present
Wrapped in cardboard
Tied with string

To him it meant everything
To you it was nothing

Weirdos

We sat together
In the crowd
Looking and listening
To the fool who was a genius
There was an empty seat next to us
And a hairy man came and sat
He smelled like wet dog
But had a camera and took photos
Then he left and we were alone again
In the crowd
And the fool who was a genius played on
Until his wife said stop
It was late and time for bed

Blasted Bulb

Damned bright spark light
Caught me reading
When I shouldn't be
So what does it do?
Goes and turns off on me
Just like that
One minute all white
The next all black
Oh the power

The Wild-Wild West

Every day's a gold rush
And you can't trust no-one
Coz they're all double-negatives
And hanging's a spectator sport
And writing's for tombstones
And real men down whiskey
And everyone's your friend
And its drinks all round

The gunslinger's in the belltower
And women hike up their skirts
And wear boots over fishnets
But it's not like the movies
Where the sheriffs aren't crooked
And the villains all don black
And everyone's your friend
And its drinks all round

It's a dry argument in a dustbowl
And you can't take a bath
Coz the town's got no water
So you wash once a month
With a jug and a basin
And the bedbugs don't mind
And everyone's your friend
And its drinks all round

The preacher's daughter's no virgin
Lucky your horse knows the way
Coz you're a wreck in a desert

And the flowers are all cactus
And your hat's full of holes
From all those near misses
And everyone's your friend
And its drinks all round

Yeah everyone's your friend
And its drinks all round

Little Lamb

I am wolf
In shepherd's clothing
I see ewe
Little lamb
My long tongue
Drips …
With anticipation
Diamonds for ewe
Just one taste
And lick of fleece
Feel my rough
On your soft
Pink white skin
My plan …
To de-flock
And chase ewe
Into submission
Through blood red eyes
With ears pricked
I lust & listen
Beneath my panting
Your little heart bleats
And for one mad second
Ewe is mine
I show mercy
But fear
Takes ewe from me
Fleeing fast
Ewe scampers away
Don't look back

In case ewe stumbles
And if ewe do
Will only see
I do not follow
I merely stay
Where I am
Entranced ...
By ewe

Out of Sync

I'm way out of sync
Unable to think
Maybe it's the drink
There must be a link
It could be you
It should be you
I don't have a clue
Now that we're through
I'm way out of sync
Now that we're through
Now that we're through
Now that we're through
I'm here on the brink
All because of you
Book me in the clink
I might need a shrink
I might need two
But they're not you
No they're not you
I just don't know
Why you had to go
And leave me
I just don't know
It all seems so slow
Nothing moves me
No nothing moves me
Now it's all for show
There's no inner glow
To warm me
I wish it wasn't so

Confusing
I wish it wasn't so
Fucking amusing
To all of you

Guide Me?

Will you guide me to the other side?
Will you whisper in my ear?
Or will you show me in my mind?
The secret path to take me clear,
Through the minefield, through the mire,
Through the corpses, through the fire,
Will you take me, be my guide?
And not forsake me because I lied,
Will you hide me from my fears?
Or will you drown me in your tears?
Will you free me from their sneers?
Will you drag me past the peers?
Or will you just deceive me?
And go off and leave me where I lie,
And not disturb my sleeping,
And just ignore their weeping when I die,
And after will you come back for me?
Even though I was a liar,
Will you take me through the wire?
Will you remember how I loved you?
Or will you think of how I doubted and mistrusted?
When you gave me all you had to give,
Will you wake me from my slumber?
Or will you deny me a reason to live?
Will that be your judgement for one crime too many?
And if there were any hope of acquittal,
Would it be dashed by my committal?
Or will I be too crazy to know?
And in the end just refuse to go

The River & the Sun

She is from and of water
Her thoughts are a stream
When she is filled
She reaches out and touches
She divides and conquers
She is the water of Cleopatra
Old as the dawn
Fresh as youth dew
She flows like a melody
Saturating the senses
And she gives everything
Down to her last drop
And her lord loves her
For all that she is
Her graceful beauty
Her magic sparkle
Even her brooding darkness
The way she bathes in herself
Calmly reflecting his golden gaze
She is aware of his powers
Yet shows not a ripple
She is cool as the night
But touched by his warmth
Feeling it gently flow through her
And when she stretches
Laying naked before him
Her skin shimmers
And her depths dazzle
Her jewels are blinding
And he is a lustful king

He would have her only for him
She is flattered and seduced
By his majestic devotion
And his eye only for her
As he slowly takes her
She knows his desire
She stirs and surges
He lifts her like a misty veil
And carries his virgin bride
Across his reaping threshold
And she anoints him
With exquisite perfumed oils
And she is purely spent
He is humbled by her
And they are a dream
When they wake
He is a thief
And she is wiser

Two Unconnected Things

It's about you, and it's about me
Two unconnected things
I'm over you, and I'm a liar
So why do I still, think about you every day?
And wish you'd come, and stay
Or go forever, and just say never
It was so nice the way, when we were apart
Each day, we'd look for each other, in the usual places
And remember, the funny things about our faces
And it will never, be the same
And I just can't, speak your name, again
Because it hurts too much, and I miss your touch
And I always will
No matter how much, I try to forget you
And I'll never ever, get over you
But what do I know?
I'm just a fool, who thinks too much?
And feels too much, and gets things wrong
Too many times, so many times
I've just lost track, and want you back
But know you're gone, for good this time
And won't come back, and never will
And it's my fault and your fault too
And you're still gone, and there's no way back
And you'll move on, and I'll pretend
And you will mend, and I'll pretend
It's not the end
I'm over you, and I'm such a liar.

Tapped

Hush …
It's only me
Your little tap
You touch me
Twist my knobs
Turn me on
And off again
Deep sigh …
Drip, drip, drip
I run for you
Hot and cold
Mostly warm
Your hands are soft
I like the lather
It smells nice
Drip, drip, drip
But the others
Who come and go
And just use us
Their hands are hard
They hurt me
And you too
I know they do
I've heard the sounds
Seen the blood
Drip, drip, drip
They soap and scrub
But can't wash away
Those sins that stain
And when I can

I burn them good
I scold their skin
We hate them
Mirror and me
She's my friend too
Just like you
She gets all misty
When we steam up
Drip, drip, drip
She tells me things
How you look
About your smile
The way you cry
And frown at times
Your hair plays tricks
And when you laugh
We do too - with you
So much sometimes
My washers jump
And mirror shimmers
And you both vibrate
We love you friend
Drip, drip, drip

Robert Gray

Like a nervous
Thirsty bird
He perched
Ginger crested
Eyes ablaze
Beak open
Feathers frayed
Thin legs
Clasped together
Flock gathered
All proud
And preening
And cackling
And calling
His answer
A song
On a breeze
So calming
Outside
He is summer
Inside
He is autumn

Bambi

It is night and the jungle lives
Excited monkeys chatter
Birds call and answer
A full moon colours leaves trees grasses - green
A brownish mist rises, thick from the earth
A musty smell wafts through ferns palms
Spider webs stretch heavy with insects
Thirsty mosquitoes hang in the heat
The backdrop - a veil of black
A doe-eyed deer creeps cautiously into a clearing
A city of eyes, look on, afraid to blink
The deer meanders, alone, lost
Breathing slows
Heartbeats synchronize
Noise tails off
Cross-hairs focus
Silence
Then the quick flick of a switch
And a great bright light makes day from night
Shocked, dazed
The little fawn freezes in hot white fear
Three hard fingers squeeze triggers
Raw instinct sets in, the deer thinks to bolt
Its knees wobble, and trembling, it stumbles
Slowly falling like a floating feather
And crumples into the ground
The sound of gunfire echoes around and dies
A wailing cry rings out
Another and another
Until a frenzied cacophony rages from the boughs

And not a hunter is heard
As they silently drag the fresh lifeless form
And the blood runs free still warm as it flows
Over grass and leaves and sticks like paint
To moss and clay on the soft moist floor
Then quick as they came they are gone again
And it is dark once more

Street Music

The city's his sheet music and lights his notes
And at the end of every line there's a bar
Where rain pisses razorblades on a cat tin roof
And he punches drunk through fresh chilled mist
With nothing but an old rolled blanket of shame
Steel wool beard rust stained and frozen with guilt
And he smells like a corpse down from the cross
And his holy mitts shake for no reason except habit
And his mind won't remember questions or answers
But somehow his lips shape words when needed
He knows it's a lie but the truth just the same
Can you spare me a dollar or two?
Can you mister anything will do?
My friend little sister anything will help
Get me back to my family my wife and kid
So long without me I miss them so much
Show me some kindness in a world without justice
And someday someway I will reward you
Thankyou kind sir thankyou dear lady
May angels from heaven bless you this day?
I'll remember you well in our last hours of judgement
I'll remember you well if I'm called as a witness
For though I may seem like the scum from the sewer
I'll have you know I'm the King of the Turds!

Too Many Questions

How many hours in a lifetime?
How many thoughts to go mad?
How many drinks make a drunkard?
How many whores have been had?
How many drops in an ocean?
How many lines in the sand?
How many stones in a mountain?
How many boys make a man?
How many spots make a leopard?
How many clouds make a storm?
How many lies make a farce?
How many deaths will we mourn?
How many bugs in a virus?
How many tolls in a bell?
How many devils in heaven?
How many angels in hell?
How many sins make a sinner?
How many souls will we sell?

In My Mind

In my mind
Thoughts were falling
In my mind
They felt the sky
In my mind
Words were weeping
In my mind
They said goodbye

In Her Garden

That night
She took them all in
A shamble of strangers
And shone them a garden
The old warned of doubt
But lied
The young showed veins
Pulsing with truth
As her friend shared her bosom
She the enchantress
Collected their souls
The speaker stroked through
His father's thick ether
And her golden boy
Plucked his harp full of hope
His soft furry friend
Purring along
The ghost of Othello
Burned like a Caesar
And two sons of madness
Confused egos with halos
While lost Magdalenes
Sang sad distant dirges
By the fading light
Of Kafka

Crimes by Starlight

And she visited
Like it was old times
And they were nervous
Like it was old times
But the kisses
Were deep
And untroubled
And it should have stopped there
But it hadn't
And his mistake
Was hers
And they were criminals
And they were
Just right
But broken
And the moon
And all the stars
Were just right
But broken
And he smiled
Like life would never end
And she smiled
Because she was happy
And life
Seemed like
Death
Again

Beautiful Things

I need to let you know
In case you've forgotten
Or never realized to begin with
That you're all beautiful
I'm not just saying it
I really mean it
Let me try and explain
You see, every day
On TV and at work
There's all this horror
So whenever I get out
And escape from it all
And I'm blessed with time
To pause and look
Sometimes I get to really see
And if I'm very lucky
I watch with wonder
As everyday things come alive
I've always had a sentimental streak
I become attached to things
Like my old second-hand cars
With all their problems
And broken bits
And parts that don't work
After years of neglect
Yeah, I talk to them
Give them genders
Names and personalities
And begin to love them
Like family and friends

I grieve when they go
Because they're a part of me
And I never really forget them
Then newer ones come along
And I fall for them too
I give them attention
But over time
I start taking them for granted
And as I get older
I realize what I'm doing
So I make an effort
And find time for them
And they're good to me
And we're happy together
And when I sit outside
And the light is just right
They appear young again
All clean and shiny
Like the first day we met
And we touch each other
In my mind
And we seem relaxed
I guess that's contentment
So I thank God
And look to the sky
And it's always beautiful
Even on the worst days
When the Sun's unhappy
And it seems like
He's trying to fry us all
Even then if we're honest
The blue is still beautiful

So when I look
At all you weeds and flowers
I think ...
What a magnificent garden
Full of variety and colour
And I think ...
How lucky am I?

So Write

Just write
And it will be
Just right
Not for critics
Afraid to live
Not for publishers
Afraid to print
Write for you and
Hearts that think
And pure pages
Thirsty for ink
Forget about faults
And be free
Share with us
Help us feel
Help us see
Just write
And let it be
Just right

Last Wishes

Do not bury me
I fear the slithering worms

Lay me on a bed of hot coals
And burn me well

Scatter my ashes
In a garden by the sea

Come visit when you can
And remember me

Haiku

summer rain
droplets glisten
air sweetens

old library
so quiet
and thoughtful

willy wag tail
twists in time
with sprinkler

without knowing
I hide the keys
from myself

I leave the shop
with everything
except what I need

missing you
I hear tapping at window
hello rain bird

she spreads her fishnets
and is satisfied
he's quite a catch

crevasse of her arse
and hidden valleys
I must explore

bees
earnestly humming away
bees

footprints in the snow
I follow cold and alone
walking in circles

homing pigeons
under the bridge
nowhere to go

wrapped in crepe paper
her last Christmas present
cradled as she sleeps

Anzac Day
marchers get younger
medals grow heavier

religiously
I park outside the church
one day I'll go in

he looked to his God
who looked to his God
and so on ...

sunlight beckons
swim up
swim up

Acknowledgements

Thanks to my family and friends for their support and encouragement - especially my daughter Felicity for first printing this book, and my friend Brahms for her inspiration.

Also to Creatrix, Famous Reporter, WritingRaw, Cottonmouth, dotdotdash, Paper Wasp and Underground Writers for taking chances and publishing many of these poems.

Finally to my fellow writers from the Katharine Susannah Prichard Writers Centre, WA Poets Inc, and Perth Poetry Club for listening, sharing and loving poetry.

www.ingramcontent.com/pod-product-compliance
Lightning Source LLC
Chambersburg PA
CBHW061504040426
42450CB00008B/1484